C000063105

i
c
o
p
e

Copyright © 2018 Brian Alan Ellis
All rights reserved.
Typesetting by Janice Lee
Cover Design by Olivia Croom
ISBN - 978-1-948700-11-5

THE ACCOMPLICES:
A Civil Coping Mechanisms Book

For more information, find CCM at:

http://copingmechanisms.net

SAD
LAUGHTER

**A Totally Unessential and
Demotivational Guide
to Reading, Writing and
Publishing**

BY **BRIAN ALAN ELLIS**

Contents

For those about to eat at a restaurant alone and pretend to read a book while actually thinking about personal shortcomings/demons/ death, we salute you!

"If you're a young writer looking to be monetarily successful, spend more time making connections than on working on anything. Also, make your books a certain length, add a clear 'narrative' and/or 'twist' and just overall make sure you view the reader as a baby looking for a toy."

– Sam Pink

★ ★ ★

"If it sounds like writing, I rewrite it."

– Elmore Leonard

★ ★ ★

"If you have any young friends who aspire to become writers, the second greatest favor you can do them is to present them with copies of *The Elements of Style*. The first greatest, of course, is to shoot them now, while they're happy."

– Dorothy Parker

Making Art is Completely Worthless Most of the Time
An Introduction

> "Told my publisher I'd get this manuscript to him as soon as possible and he said, 'Fuck yeah, this is going to be a big one,' and I immediately pictured that pile of dinosaur shit from the movie *Jurassic Park*."
>
> **– Brian Alan Ellis**

When you die, you might go down into the eternal flames of Hell and have to read craft essays on how to construct perfect sentences that pop. The devil will have a dry erase board and Ann Lamott quotes will be all over that thing. Pull quote after pull quote from *Bird By Bird*. There will even be other writers there who will be on fire and as they burn they will repeat that Stephen King quote, "The road to Hell is paved with adverbs." Haha, isn't this a fucking hoot?

When you die though, most likely, nothing will happen. You're not going to suffer. You're not gonna get your just rewards either. But! There's a chance that all those small press books you put out will suddenly find a wider audience. Something to look forward to. I'm gonna get so goddamn rich once I'm dead.

The artist Brian Alan Ellis gets out of bed. He hasn't showered in four days. He lives in a collapsing punk house, with his cat. He has on a Carly Rae Jepsen t-shirt and his Virgin Mobile flip phone is ringing like crazy. He answers. It's his literary agent. The agent says, "Brian, here's the deal. You can't do this book with Civil Coping Mechanisms. Please, please, please. You have to break your contract with Seidlinger and get the book into Alfred A. Knopf's hands." Brian thinks about it. He looks around the room at the garbage piled up everywhere. The cat's litter box is overflowing. He says, "Wild." The agent says, "Another thing, Jake Gyllenhaal is attached to the shoot now. Jake is playing you. He's doing 3600 sit ups a day to get in shape. Kettlebell workouts." Brian laughs, hangs up the phone, and walks out into the house without his underwear on.

The tables are covered in crushed beer cans and empty prescription drug bottles. His roommates are having group sex with a prostitute who is wearing a purple wig. Brian walks past them all and into the kitchen, where he cracks eight eggs into a glass and drinks them raw just like Rocky Balboa.

Today you might see a link online to a website with the top ten umbrellas featured in literary fiction. You might click an interview where a debut novelist casually drops the truth bomb: "I didn't think I could write the great American novel. But then I sailed around the world on my granddaddy's schooner." You might get a notification on Twitter that you've been followed by Bret Easton Ellis. Holy shit! No, wait, it's Brian Alan Ellis. Even cooler.

The artist Brian Alan Ellis puts his pants and shoes on and walks out into the Florida heat towards the restaurant where he sells beer and nachos to normal people who

14

aren't pretentious pieces of shit. Who don't think, as E.L. Doctorow says, "[Writing is] like driving a car at night: you never see further than your headlights, but you can make the whole trip that way." Wait a minute, who is E.L. Doctorow? Who cares? Oh, he wrote a book called *Ragtime*. The people at the table say, "Another order of boneless wings. Hurry up."

Brian puts the order in with the line cook, and slumps against the wall and tweets: *My literary goal may or may not be to publish as many relatively unsuccessful books in a 5-year span as possible. Think I'm up to about 11 or 12 so far.* He presses send. Within 9 hours he will have reviewed 3 "likes" on the tweet.

After his shift, Brian walks to the liquor store and buys a fifth of whiskey. He drinks it alone in his room, watching pro wrestling clips on YouTube. Later he tweets: *Just spent 8 hours working on 3 different manuscripts. Writing sucks but at least it's a distraction from waiting 8 hours on a text/phone call from someone that never arrives.* And it's true. Making art is completely worthless most of the time, but it is the best distraction going when you are lonely. The cat is crying and Brian says, "Come here." The cat jumps up on his lap and he pets the cat for a while. The cat meows and Brian understands it. It's the cat's way of saying, "Are you alright, Brian? You seem really depressed and I'm worried about you. Are you going to kill yourself?" Brian smiles and says, "No kitty, no I'm not. You know why? Because I'm coping."

– Bud Smith, 2017

SAD LAUGHTER

1. Poetry Readings Are Like Really Weird AA Meetings

You may or may not hope to one day publish a book implanted with a sound chip that when opened plays a 20-second clip of "Ya'll Ready for This (*Space Jam* Theme)."

★ ★ ★

A Goodreads shelf titled "I'll Get Around to It If Nothing Better Comes Along."

★ ★ ★

Shout-out to any critic who has ever reviewed one of your books by academically calling you a low-life scumbag.

★ ★ ★

HOT LIT TIP: When you die, make sure all of your unpublished work can be found zipped inside one of those Scrote'n'Tote bags. [Google it.]

★ ★ ★

Having a job where wearing a paper hat is required vs. Folding your MFA degree into a paper hat and wearing it around your neighborhood while crying/screaming.

★ ★ ★

Finalize your MFA semen samples and chill?

★ ★ ★

Poet-in-Residence @ the corner of broke and alone.

★ ★ ★

Who are your favorite writers that haven't gone to ~~college or have an MFA~~ summer camp and/or had to share a room with their grandma until they were 18 years old?

★ ★ ★

So you sold your first novel for a VHS copy of *Road Trip*, so what?

★ ★ ★

When other authors recommend how-to writing books to you on Goodreads, it's like WTF they trying to say?

★ ★ ★

Poetry reading where you pretend to fall asleep while reading and a marching band (hired) followed by a parent with a screaming child (not hired) shows up but you stay "asleep."

★ ★ ★

Poet-in-Residence @ the corner of Know Your Role Blvd. and Jabroni Dr.

★ ★ ★

14 Must-Read Books This Year, None of Them Yours

★ ★ ★

A book like *Infinite Jest* but instead of having to read footnotes, you are directed to pull up several YouTube tutorials.

★ ★ ★

What they don't tell you about running a small press: Fat checks will just magically drop into your lap as you're finally being invited onto Rupi Kaur's private jet.

★ ★ ★

Customer: In some circles they call me the poet laureate of the pre-packaged gas station sandwich.

Barista: Yeah, whatever, but can I have an actual name for the cup?

★ ★ ★

Author picture where the author is photographed going up for thirds at a Golden Corral buffet.

★ ★ ★

Book launch party where you and the audience literally try launching copies of your book into a garbage can placed at the far end of the room using a Medieval-style catapult contraption.

★ ★ ★

Join ISIS > Create an "author" Facebook page

★ ★ ★

Can anyone really stomach *Reader's Digest?* [Cue *Seinfeld* theme music.]

★ ★ ★

Shout-out to all the writers whose books you promised to write comprehensive reviews for but then just threw some bullshit up on Goodreads.

★ ★ ★

Dreamed you invented a font that could only be deciphered by literate drunks.

★ ★ ★

Convince yourself that literary journals that only consider postal submissions are just trying to piss writers off, and like it. Like it a lot.

★ ★ ★

Updated version of *The Elements of Style* where you're encouraged to simplify words and descriptive action by using helpful emojis.

★ ★ ★

Pen name goals: Proseanne Barr

★ ★ ★

Social media is the preferred art form used by writers to remind themselves and others that "Hey, I'm a writer," besides just sobbing uncontrollably into their hands in front of their pets.

★ ★ ★

Poetry reading at an EDM rave.

★ ★ ★

Writers' residency where you stay where you are but you stop paying rent. The residency ends when your landlord calls the police.

★ ★ ★

Miller High Life > Arthur Miller

★ ★ ★

Would be cool to win a literary award that was actually just a sock, or a Big Johnson t-shirt rednecks used to wear at your high school, or maybe even a freshly dug-up Ghostface mask from the movie *Scream* that was buried in 1997.

★ ★ ★

HOT LIT TIP: 1) Ask writers to watch the Guns N' Roses "November Rain" music video, 2) have them write about it, 3) use what they write as blurbs to your book.

★ ★ ★

"Blurbs? Where we're going, we don't need blurbs..."

★ ★ ★

When the folks publishing your novel call you a bastard in an e-mail and you shrug and nod agreeably because you are one/never met your biological dad.

★ ★ ★

All great love stories should cover at least two of the following subjects: 1) Greyhound, 2) blow jobs from crackheads, 3) the first Suicidal Tendencies LP.

★ ★ ★

Reminder: Books by Norman Mailer are only enjoyable if you repeatedly stab them with a penknife/don't bother reading them.

★ ★ ★

If on a Winter's Night a Blues Traveler #90sABook

★ ★ ★

♪ I was looking for an adjunct MFA teaching job and I found an adjunct MFA teaching job and heaven knows I'm miserable now ♪

★ ★ ★

The Beets (as in the band from the Nickelodeon *Doug* cartoon) > The Beats (as in the "Generation")

★ ★ ★

Submission fees are a way of finding out who all the sad, desperate writers are by trapping them.

★ ★ ★

Book review/blurb where you only comment on the tone/attitude/style the writer used when asking you to review/blurb their book.

★ ★ ★

A literary podcast where everything the host and/or writer says is interrupted by audio clips of WWE Superstar Stone Cold Steve Austin saying, "What?"

★ ★ ★

A "Collected Works" comprised of all the times your life fell apart and you had to move back in with your parents to regroup.

★ ★ ★

Writing is like trying to make sense of an inside joke you have with yourself but haha joke's on you 'cause the joke is more sad than funny.

★ ★ ★

A Reading Series of Unfortunate Events

★ ★ ★

"Bullfighting is lit af fam! —Ernest Hemingway

★ ★ ★

If your author photo doesn't make you look like you're
a villain from *Scott Pilgrim vs. the World*, then you're
probably doing it wrong.

★ ★ ★

Is there a pop song about walking a mile to the post office
in 37 degree weather to mail out small press paperbacks,
and if not, how come?

★ ★ ★

*Submission guidelines: Would totally consider your work but we're
completely overcome by depression and self-loathing so check back,
maybe?*

★ ★ ★

Just got dumped? No worries. It's good to be back to just
you, your pet, and those boxes of books you may or may
not sell at the next reading you don't really want to be at.

★ ★ ★

Not only are business cards a lot cheaper to publish than
books, they are a lot easier to write/design/edit etc. etc. so
why not say fuck it and go into the business card business?

★ ★ ★

"Everything was retweeted and nothing hurt."—Kurt
Vonnegut

★ ★ ★

Do poets ever accuse other poets of stealing their shitty similes, or is joke theft just a stand-up comedy thing?

★ ★ ★

Who are your favorite writers that ~~haven't gone to college or have an MFA~~ could beat *Super Mario Brothers* for NES without losing any lives?

★ ★ ★

Some people collect vintage typewriters to show others that "Yes, I am a writer." However, discarded fast food to-go bags and other random trash works just as well.

★ ★ ★

Ernest Hemingway < Ernest P. Worrell

★ ★ ★

MFA in being a fly on the wall to your own undoing.

★ ★ ★

"Look, we'll consider publishing your book if you don't mind us putting a picture of ALF on the cover."

★ ★ ★

"Keep Books Dangerous" AKA "Keep Authors Poor, Angry, and Marginalized."

2. One-Act Play Set in the Prepaid Phone Aisle at a Dollar General

Your main literary aspiration should involve getting too drunk and then having to be physically removed from the KGB Bar in New York City.

★ ★ ★

Writer Panics about Finishing Latest Manuscript on Time, Like Anyone Actually Gives a Shit

★ ★ ★

Reminder: The CIA started *The Paris Review*, *The New Yorker* is Mafia-affiliated, and *The NY Times Book Review* is written by highly gifted fourth graders.

★ ★ ★

[Insert number] Writers to Watch Have a Complete Meltdown on Facebook While Threatening to Delete Their Account in [insert year]

★ ★ ★

Let's see how your literary "brand" is doing, shall we? *shakes Magic 8 Ball*

★ ★ ★

If you're a publisher and are not rejecting submissions like someone playing a next gen shooter then what the hell are you even doing in life?

★ ★ ★

The Poet Laureate of hooking up with someone they shouldn't be hooking up with.

★ ★ ★

Do you even "Works at Writer/Author" on Facebook, bro?

★ ★ ★

When finding out the editor who rejected your work does yoga, let that feeling of relief wash over you.

★ ★ ★

Reminder: Feel obliged to tell authors that you're just not down to fuck... with their books.

★ ★ ★

Q: Tell me about your writing process...

A: I'm glad you asked... umm... *nervous laughter followed by devastating head-butt*

★ ★ ★

Opening line to an existential novel you'd really like to one day write/read/abandon:

After beating Mike Tyson's Punch-Out!! *I found that there was nothing left to prove and that my life had relinquished all purpose.*

★ ★ ★

So you sold your first novel for Burger King Groupons which you later found out had expired, so what?

★ ★ ★

Literature can be its own kind of prison. Pretty sure Creed's Scott Stapp said that.

★ ★ ★

The Poet Laureate of complete and utter dankness.

★ ★ ★

HOT LIT TIP: Give up writing short stories and novels. Write poems instead. That way, your work can be less relevant *and* less profitable. Win.

★ ★ ★

You may or may not be 100% uninterested in any book with a title ending or beginning in *Book 1.*

★ ★ ★

"So you *didn't* like the story about ALF I submitted? Damn it, just be honest with me!"

* * *

Recommended Summer Beach Reads for When You're Drowning in Life vs. Recommended Summer Beach Reads for When You're Literally Drowning at the Beach

* * *

Navigating the literary community is like playing a shitty *Sims* game where the goal is to beef up your CV, make a bunch of fake friends, and to try to not kill your brand/ starve to death due to lack of validation/money.

* * *

MFA in assembling peanut butter and jelly sandwiches.

* * *

Instagram account where parents of childless authors are pictured lovingly cradling blanket-wrapped copies of their kids' newly published books in a hospital setting.

* * *

You may or may not be forever searching for the literary equivalent to that one Ugly Kid Joe song. You know the one.

* * *

Pen name goals: Axl Prose

* * *

Writers giving advice is like the drunk parent who lectured

you about responsibility after they were late picking you up from somewhere.

★ ★ ★

Preferring matte over glossy because when you snort drugs off of a book cover, it's best to not see a shadowy reflection of what you've become.

★ ★ ★

Because I couldn't find a date to Bogey Lowenstein's party. #WhyIWrite

★ ★ ★

Poets, please stop writing long poems. That's just more of something nobody really wants.

★ ★ ★

Poem you'd write if you were a ghost trying to scare someone:

BOO!

★ ★ ★

Obituary: *He/she is survived by his/her Want-to-Read/ Currently-Reading Goodreads shelf.*

★ ★ ★

The Poet Laureate of whatever bullshit job they work at.

★ ★ ★

#TFW people simultaneously post on both their regular and "author" Facebook pages and you get stressed choosing which to "like" and so you don't bother with either.

★ ★ ★

New book by Tommy Lee > new book by Harper Lee

★ ★ ★

"While My ~~Guitar~~ Kindle Gently Weeps"

★ ★ ★

You've seen the best minds of your generation ironically use the phrase "I saw the best minds of my generation..." maybe a couple times, who knows?

★ ★ ★

Go Ask Alice in Chains #90sABook

★ ★ ★

"Oooooh, 'best-sellers list'! I thought you'd said 'Ben Kweller's list'... My bad! LOL Fuck that guy, right?"

★ ★ ★

receives text

Hey, can you set up a reading for me? I have a new poetry chapbook out and...

flushes phone down the toilet

★ ★ ★

The Poet Laureate of Judas Priest references.

★ ★ ★

Reminder: The best thing about running a Goodreads book giveaway contest is getting to judge/stalk the winners via their Goodreads profiles.

★ ★ ★

Doing readings/podcasts may or may not be how you suffer for your art.

★ ★ ★

"Freeze, this is a literary citizen's arrest!"

★ ★ ★

Stuck between a rock and a weekly poetry slam.

★ ★ ★

Yeah, sex is cool but have you tried rejecting someone's writing?

★ ★ ★

Need a strong quote to open your book with? Try:

"Hey yo!"—WWF Superstar Razor Ramon

★ ★ ★

People who name their pets after famous authors are LOL so why not name your cat Meowncé, instead?

★ ★ ★

Hell is open submissions.

3. Articles about Writing Tools for Writers vs. Articles about Writers Who Are Tools

A "Collected Works" that's really whatever is left in the bathroom sink after giving yourself a really questionable haircut.

* * *

Sext: *I'll blurb yr book so hard you'll forget that book blurbs are just ego-stroking bs publishers perpetuate & that nothing really matters*

* * *

Poetry reading where only box wine and Lunchables are served as refreshments.

* * *

So you sold your first novel for a dog-eared copy of the *Playboy* with late WWE Superstar Chyna on the cover, so what?

* * *

Writers' residency where you stay on your buddy's couch after being evicted and then observe his/her horrified reactions to seeing how a writer actually exists in this world.

* * *

An energy drink called LIT that has real intense literature on the cans as opposed to the non-intense literature on Chipotle to-go bags/soft drink cups, or maybe just real intense pictures of the '90s rock band Lit.

* * *

Q: Do you have a time of day when you're feeling most creative?

A: Not really. Finding the time of day when I'm not feeling lazy is what I'm most concerned about, and I really don't think this time of day actually exists. Oh well.

* * *

Poetry reading where you read poems using a Virgin Mobile flip phone purchased at a Dollar General before Obama was president AKA your actual phone.

* * *

Reminder: Pictures of Carson McCullers when she's drunk should be one of your main literary influences.

* * *

Might be cooler if the literary community was split into two distinct groups: "Greasers" and "Socs."

* * *

Who needs physical/emotional human love when you have a wildly insignificant writing career to comfort you? *hyperventilates into Wendy's to-go bag*

★ ★ ★

The Poet Laureate of getting jumped outside of a Waffle House at 4 AM.

★ ★ ★

General response while browsing another "Most Exciting Books of [insert year]" list: Meh.

★ ★ ★

"What books ya'll reading? JK haha don't care!"

★ ★ ★

Author photo where the author looks deathly afraid of impending irrelevancy.

★ ★ ★

"Secret warm-up gig" before poetry reading that's just you crying/screaming in the backseat of a car while punching yourself in face.

★ ★ ★

Picture a dramatic, heart-tugging Bruce Springsteen-style song but instead of it being about workers laid off from industrial factories closing, it'll be about all your precious stories/poems that were accepted but never published

because the literary journals they were supposed to be in
ended up folding prematurely.

★ ★ ★

Submission guidelines: We accept poetry haha JK

★ ★ ★

Making a book trailer? Can't emphasize enough the
importance of having lots of footage of Chuck Norris
roundhouse-kicking cokeheads in the face.

★ ★ ★

Poet in residence @ what used to be a Spec's Music location.

★ ★ ★

Fantasy that your books are being taught in schools that
aesthetically resemble the school from *Saved by the Bell*.

★ ★ ★

"I Live in A Car" by the UK Subs > your poetry, most likely

★ ★ ★

LiveJournal probably doesn't get enough credit for its
development of terrible writers.

★ ★ ★

A good method to stay motivated while working on your
novel is to keep telling yourself, "Well, at least it's better

than that shitty zine I did 10 years ago."

★ ★ ★

What's the deal with literary journals that have a "mission statement"? Like, do the editors put on camo and then arm themselves with shitty poems before heading to some foreign country to save POWs? [Cue *Seinfeld* theme music.]

★ ★ ★

"Look, we'll consider publishing your book if you don't mind adding '666' to the title, k?"

★ ★ ★

A "Collected Works" comprised of whatever is found under your couch cushions when you try desperately retrieving that M&M you dropped.

★ ★ ★

Tonight, during WWE *Monday Night Raw*, let's all officially announce our retirement from indie publishing.

★ ★ ★

Twilight Zone episode where a writer has a nagging suspicion that their writing is as awful as everyone else's writing.

★ ★ ★

The Best Boring Writer Asking another Boring Writer Questions about Boring Writing of [insert year]

★ ★ ★

Practice your eye rolls by following writers on social media.

★ ★ ★

Trigger warning: contains the phrase "For all intents and purposes…"

★ ★ ★

The Wayans Brothers Karamazov #90sABook

★ ★ ★

"If your script doesn't have at least two cafeteria food fight scenes then sorry, not interested."

★ ★ ★

Reminder: There is a special hell for writers who use #amwriting and that hell is called Twitter.

★ ★ ★

Nobel Prize in Literature for owning Internet trolls on message boards.

★ ★ ★

#TFW your book has so many trigger warnings that you have to unfollow it on Tumblr.

★ ★ ★

Dream where Andy Kaufman narrates your audio book, only he sounds like WWE Superstar Triple H.

* * *

Literary journal called *Dear Loser*, where everyone accepted (or rejected) is a loser.

* * *

"The fact that there is a tournament for books is a pretty pathetic affair," and that's probably coming from an adult who still watches professional wrestling.

* * *

#amcopyingandpastingtweetsintoamanuscript

VS.

#amwriting

* * *

The Poet Laureate of gluing thrift store shoes back together.

* * *

HOT LIT TIP: This Christmas, put your Kindle to good use by snorting drugs off of it.

* * *

ATTN snobby academic writers: there's nothing wrong with making books out of glue, tape, staples and scissors and then selling them from out of the trunk of your car. (If you have a car.)

4. NO BOOK BLURB, NO CRY

An Inspirational/Crazy Informative Guide to Proper Book Blurbage

"[This book] will fry up some prose eggs in your ol' brain pan."

★ ★ ★

"[This writer] is the kind of poet whose madness and how [he/she] exorcises that madness is a thing of dark brilliance one can admire from afar but if you ever let [him/her] crash at your house for a few days [he/she] would scare the living shit out of you."

★ ★ ★

"[This writer] can fix your pipes and your roofing but [his/her] book of durable, brick-layered stories can also fix your mind plumbing, too."

★ ★ ★

"[This book] sends a roundhouse kick to your funny bone before blowing it up. Disagree? Then I don't consider you a person; you are a terrorist towards good taste."

★ ★ ★

"Reading [this book] is like waking up to find a bloody horsehead in bed with you and then screaming but not screaming because you're repulsed but because you've actually discovered a fresh way to look at life and it's amazing."

★ ★ ★

"[This writer] definitely has a way with words—they aren't written; they're kicked and fondled before being splattered across the page like a dead, wet dog."

★ ★ ★

"[He/She] is the type of writer you'd let crash at your apartment and then wake up to find they've murdered your pets and then turned them into dancing puppets that are now lip-synching to all your favorite Debbie Gibson cassingles, so yeah, a real party animal."

★ ★ ★

"[This book] takes readers on an uncompromising funhouse ride of damaged people attractions."

★ ★ ★

"[This writer] is the type of poet who will put [his/her] head through a plate glass window just to make killer poetry out of [his/her] face."

★ ★ ★

"[This book] is a brave and poignant look into a person's mind as they struggle to exist in a world where Hulkamania is generally not the strongest force in the universe and we are all in danger of being crushed by a 500-pound giant hailing from parts unknown."

★ ★ ★

"[This book] is recommended for anyone who knows how to read."

★ ★ ★

"[He/She] is the kind of writer clever enough to moonlight as a lawyer/sociopath capable of freaking out a table full of squares by using hella unassuming methods, so yeah, a delightful talent."

★ ★ ★

"[This writer] writes like a sadistically imaginative child who plays house by burning down the house."

★ ★ ★

"[This book is] a coming-of-age fever dream [the author] carved into some Ouija board [he/she] later used to summon the spirits of David Koresh, Jesus Christ, and Richard Ramirez."

★ ★ ★

"[This writer] is like the Tombstone of frozen descriptive prose pizza."

★ ★ ★

45

"While reading [this book] you'll feel as though you've been taken hostage, stuffed and then zipped inside of [the author's] emotional baggage, which is okay because at least it's warm in there."

★ ★ ★

"[This book] is kind of like Dostoevsky's *The Brothers Karamazov* meets Soundgarden's *Badmotorfinger*, or maybe like *The Notebook* meets *Re-Animator*, I don't fucking know."

★ ★ ★

"[This writer] is like Sissy Spacek in the movie *Carrie* when they dump pig blood on her but instead of setting the prom on fire [he/she] ignites your thoughts using dark and mysterious word torches."

★ ★ ★

"If the literary scene were a slammin' mosh pit, [this writer] would be commanding that shit using windmills and crazy roundhouse kicks."

★ ★ ★

"[This book's] narrative is like the music video for Van Halen's 'Right Now,' except it makes sense, and it's funny for the right reasons, and it isn't as preachy."

★ ★ ★

"[This book] is the literary equivalent of Kid Rock's dandruff."

★ ★ ★

"Though [this writer] has never won a literary award, it's quite possible they've accidentally urinated on themselves while drunk, so…"

★ ★ ★

"Crackling with powerful satanic energy, [this book] is like *When Harry Met Sally* except Harry listens to nu metal and Sally is possessed by Zuul from *Ghostbusters*, has an addiction to shitty speed, and may or may not be a juggalo."

★ ★ ★

"[He/She] is the type of writer you'd let crash at your apartment and then wake up to find naked and summoning weird spirits while kneeling in the center of some pentagram they've drawn out on your living room floor using your pet's blood, so yeah, a real pain in the ass."

★ ★ ★

"Reading [this book] is like having your emotions constantly dunked on by Shaq."

★ ★ ★

"Some authors take breaks from writing by doing yoga and going on spiritual retreats; [this author] walks to the gas station to purchase three different bags of flavored Doritos and a Chipwich. Tomayto, tomahto."

★ ★ ★

"[He/She] is the kind of writer who will pilfer a leather bomber jacket out of a garbage can and then hit the shitty neighborhood bar thinking they look real goddamn good in it, so yeah, a kindred spirit."

★ ★ ★

"[This book is] dripping with comical dark poignancy... like a bacon, egg and cheese McGriddle."

★ ★ ★

"Reading [this writer] is like getting a totally sweet hand job from someone with an MFA—someone really smart, but also someone kinda shifty, kinda dangerous."

★ ★ ★

"[This writer] is the type of person who'd eat the fries off your plate after you've gotten up to use the bathroom at Perkins, which means they're a real sneaky ass."

★ ★ ★

"Sorry, book blurb was replaced by Metallica's *St. Anger* snare drum sound."

5. WE'RE ALL GOING TO DIE SOMEDAY, SO THERE'S NO USE WASTING PRECIOUS TIME WITH ARCHAIC FORMALITIES

Proper "Submission Guidelines" Etiquette for Your Bullshit Literary Journal Nobody Really Cares About

ATTN:

Submissions are finally open (God knows why; the last issue sold like shit), so get hella stoked!

WHAT WE WANT:

Anything that's under 1000 words (you want your long shit in here? Fuck you, go try submitting to *The Believer* or whatever): flash stories, poems that don't suck, tweets, conversations, short plays, letters, rap lyrics, grocery lists, whatever. Just make it short and sweet. Also, we may be dead inside but we like to laugh. Make us laugh, motherfucker! Tell us a story we will remember through the ages. Redefine what shitty means. We're waiting.

WHAT WE DON'T WANT:

No images or artwork; we'll solicit that on our own from trained professionals (AKA friends who work for cheap). No rules; unless they're the rules we made up, in which case oh well. No fear; take fear someplace else.

DEADLINE:

Fuck it. Get your shit to us whenever. You got plenty of time. This shit might never even come out.

PAYMENT:

We won't pay you; we have our own shitty, crap-paying jobs (or are currently unemployed). What we will do is send you one paperback contributors copy, as well as a discount code to order additional paperback copies to sell from out the trunk of your car/give to all of your friends and family because, yes, you're a legit published author currently wallowing in the muck of narcissistic expression, so congratulations! (Also, we promise to not Facebook-invite you to any potential book-release events pertaining to our journal, so that's pretty dope, right?)

PROCEDURE:

We ONLY accept submissions via e-mail; Submittable is too complicated and we do whatever we can to keep the mailman off our fucking property. Also, we want you to directly PASTE your submission into the e-mail itself. We're not downloading shit. Don't even think about sending attachments. We don't get attached so why should your submission get attached? Include a bio? Sure, why not? We don't mind judging you by your accomplishments—hell, we'll probably just google you anyway. As for cover letters: don't bother; we're all going to die someday, so there's no use wasting precious time with archaic formalities.

E-MAIL:

DearLoser@gmail.com

MOST IMPORTANTLY:

Have fun!

WE LOVE YOU 4-EVER 666,

Sincerely,
The Editors

6. #amhiding > #amwriting

First rule of Write Club: You do not talk about your current word count.

★ ★ ★

Poetry reading where you read from poems taped to the inside lenses of your sunglasses i.e. cheating-ass teenagers in '80s high school movies.

★ ★ ★

The Poet Laureate of doing coke in public bathrooms.

★ ★ ★

List of Bands You Didn't Realize Got Their Names From Random Phrases in Books They Were Only Browsing Through at Barnes & Noble to Appear Hip

★ ★ ★

Perhaps you've never read Haruki Murakami but assume most people who've read Murakami haven't read James Purdy or Stephen Dixon so *Even Stevens* starring Shia LaBeouf in their face!

★ ★ ★

HOT LIT TIP: Stay humble by regularly checking your Amazon sales rankings.

★ ★ ★

Imagine a literary-themed rom-com called *He's Just Not That into Your Poetry*, or don't, whatever.

★ ★ ★

Trigger warning: "an exciting new voice."

★ ★ ★

★sees something online that might be poetry★

Oh fuck...

★quickly scrolls past★

★ ★ ★

"Well, the poetry reading was going well until people started reading their poems."

★ ★ ★

The best thing about recording an audio book is that you get to sit in something called an "isolation booth," which rules 'cause fuck people, right?

★ ★ ★

You may or may not want someone to dramatically introduce you at your next reading by shouting, "You wanted the bereft? You got the bereft! The saddest person in the world..."

★ ★ ★

Q: How would you describe your writing style?

A: I basically just copy and paste tweets and random
      Facebook posts into a word doc, which is my low-
      key way of telling "serious" writers with MFA
      degrees to go fuck themselves.

★ ★ ★

Sext: *I want you to think of the reviews section for my novel on
Amazon as my Sarahah.*

★ ★ ★

Grammar exercise:

"Everything is the worst." vs "Every thing is the worst."

★ ★ ★

Ever notice how annoying and desperate authors get after
they publish a book not too many people care about?

★ ★ ★

What sucks about opening submissions for your journal is
that you have to eventually tell all those people that their
work isn't good enough via e-mail—or do you?

★ ★ ★

The fact that Stephen King refers to himself as "Uncle
Stevie" is creepier than any of his books combined, and
that's a lot of books, yeesh!

★ ★ ★

*Notices an article titled *"Publishers Weekly's* 10 Best Linked Story Collections"*

Oh, you mean, like, novels?

★ ★ ★

Southern Gothic Lit vs. Mall Goth(ic) Lit

★ ★ ★

"'Happy Pub Day'? More like, 'Ah, Another Excuse for An Author's Narcissism and/or Anxiety to Run Amok Day,' am I right?" [Cue *Seinfeld* theme music.]

★ ★ ★

It may or may not be a good thing that touring poets don't get fucked with by cops and/or beat up by skinheads at readings i.e. '80s Black Flag shows.

★ ★ ★

Poetry reading where you read poems in your best "haunted sad girl" voice. [Extra points if you are not a haunted sad girl.]

★ ★ ★

Q: Do you have a special location or environment that you have to be in to write?

A: Usually on my back with the shades down and my pants off. No?

★ ★ ★

Catherine O'Hara > Frank O'Hara

★ ★ ★

#TFW you realize you've never, not once, properly inserted a USB thumb drive into a computer without first reversing it several times and/or just trying to force the fucking thing in there, even though you've been using said thumb drive for several years and should by now know how the physical dynamics of this piece of plastic crap should goddamn work, and you start to think it's probably just your subconscious daring you to go ahead and *break the shit, dummy, so you'll lose all your unfinished writing projects and stop fooling yourself* LOL

★ ★ ★

Poetry readings are basically just people speaking dramatically at their phones/notebooks/sheets of paper while other people politely sit and watch, maybe fantasizing about being someplace else.

★ ★ ★

Ghost on your darlings > Kill your darlings

★ ★ ★

Dream where you're writing a satirical memoir about Jeff Tweedy from Wilco's attempts at writing a novel and are really satisfied with the progress made.

★ ★ ★

#TFW finding out the poems bae wrote you were actually just lyrics to obscure Smashing Pumpkins B-sides.

* * *

Poet-in-Residence @ the sound stage where *Pee-wee's Playhouse* was filmed but only after the show got cancelled and the sound stage was gutted.

* * *

A fun thing to do: Picture late WWE Superstar Macho Man Randy Savage narrating the audio version of *A Tale of Two Cities*.

* * *

Writer Wins Humanitarian Award for Posting Contents Page of Lit Journal's New Issue Instead of Just a Direct Link to Their Own Damn Story

* * *

ATTN: Submissions are now open for this year's Best American Garbage *anthology!*

* * *

Respect if you're currently writing the literary equivalent to a moderately shitty stick-and-poke tattoo.

* * *

The Poet Laureate of sorting wet garbage.

* * *

Q: You've published a lot of books. How do you stay so prolific?

A: Yeah, functional depression seems to be going okay.

★ ★ ★

Just to be clear, whenever someone says, "Please review my books," what they're really saying is, "Please help by adding insight into my damaged psyche."

★ ★ ★

Twitter may or may not be the literary equivalent of being a mostly shitty street magician.

★ ★ ★

A story critique by people who've obviously never seen a *Die Hard* movie but are crazy into physics:

There's some good creativity in the story, but overall it needs more polish. On one of the major plot points, we all wondered the same thing: If Jimmy's already on the windshield when she peels out, wouldn't he be pushed more into the car, or possibly roll onto the roof, rather than fall under the car and get run over?

★ ★ ★

Reminder: The one good thing about self-publishing is that there isn't any pressure to do a book tour. You don't have to recoup someone else's money, so you can just stay home in your pajamas and be irrelevant. Pretty cool, huh?

7. BURY YOURSELF WITH UNUSED ISBN CODES

Titles to Books You May or May Not Hope to One Day Publish

A Portrait of the Artist as a Young Fuck Boy

★ ★ ★

Asexual Fried Bologna Sandwich Eaters from Mars: A Love Story

★ ★ ★

Bullshit Revisited: A Biography

★ ★ ★

Cuz Depression: Collected Works

★ ★ ★

That New Haunted Car Smell: A Paranormal Bromance

★ ★ ★

Pretty Sure I'm Going to Die: Essays about All the Illnesses I Googled and Thought I Had but Didn't

★ ★ ★

Mom Got Upset and Hung Up on Me and Won't Answer When I Call Her Back and Now I Want To Smash Something LOL: A Memoir

★ ★ ★

Genuine Emotional Connections Apparently Mean Nothing and Other Concerns

★ ★ ★

The Holy Grail of Completely Meaningless Bullshit: An Oral History

★ ★ ★

Death by Asphyxiation While Head is Trapped Inside of a Plastic Big Lots Bag and Other Poems

★ ★ ★

Relationships Don't Work and People Can't Fulfill You Which Is Why It Makes Perfect Sense That Someone Would Have Sex with a Parked Van: Essays

★ ★ ★

Who Dis Dick?: A Mystery

★ ★ ★

Indifferently Spooning Peanut Butter Out of a Jar and Other Traumas Sadly Manifested—Now an Exciting Audio Book!

★ ★ ★

Suicidal Self-Checkout vs. Walmart Self-Checkout: A Manifesto

★ ★ ★

An Endless Cycle of Mostly Being Miserable: A Memoir

★ ★ ★

Mom's Spaghetti: An Omnibus of Battle Raps Inspired by Eminem

★ ★ ★

A Good Man-Purse Is Hard To Find and Other Stories

★ ★ ★

Kind of Want to Bury Myself in Your Garbage and Die There Because Your Garbage Gets Me: A Love Story

★ ★ ★

Gazing Off In My Cargos and Puka Shell Necklace: Collected Broems

★ ★ ★

The Old Man and the Nintendo Wii

★ ★ ★

Fuck You, I'm Sad: Interviews and Encounters

★ ★ ★

Blah Blah Blah: An Idiot Asshole Thriller

★ ★ ★

Drunkenly Wandering Around in Search of Your Next Questionable Decision like You're a Lost Child Looking for Their Mother in a Grocery Store and Other Stories

★ ★ ★

The Heart Is a Lonely Hunter Hearst Helmsley: Flash Fiction Inspired by WWE Superstar Triple H

★ ★ ★

Like Letting Air Out of a Hope Balloon: Selected Poems

★ ★ ★

Halloween Horror Nights but It's Really Just You Spending the Month of October in Bed Alone While Compulsively Overthinking Your Many Failings and Regrets, Your Muffled Pillow Screams the Last Thing You Hear Before Finally Exhausting Yourself into Bad Sleep: A Fun Activity Guide

★ ★ ★

OMG I Gotta Tell You about This Weird Dream I Had and Other Weird Dreams You Had

★ ★ ★

Mental Illness/Self-Delusion Coupled with Fear of Death/ Irrelevancy is What Keeps Me Going: Collected Pictures of Cardboard Boxes Containing Copies of Books Authors Have Posted on Social Media to Fuel Narcissistic Literary Efforts

★ ★ ★

Lost It in the Dairy Queen Bathroom: A Sexual Awakening

★ ★ ★

What We Talk About When We Talk About Shameless Self-Promotion: The Asshole's Guide to Online Marketing

★ ★ ★

Nobody Ever Told Me I'd One Day Be This Dead Inside: Collected Facebook Account Deactivation Posts

★ ★ ★

I Swear, It's Just My Blood That's Gotten Fat: How to Empower the Garbage-Eater Within

★ ★ ★

Crying. Always Crying: A Memoir

★ ★ ★

The Unbearable Lightness of Being Your Kindle Direct Publishing Month-to-Date Unit Sales: A Survival Guide

★ ★ ★

Existential Breakdown in the Christmas Aisle at Walgreens and Other Existential Breakdowns in Other Aisles at Other Places

★ ★ ★

I Lost It at the Redbox Kiosk: A Sexual Awakening 2

★ ★ ★

Why Won't You Burn, World?: An Illustrated History

★ ★ ★

Diary of a Wimpy Grown-Ass Man

★ ★ ★

From the Outside Logging In: A Cyber Romance

★ ★ ★

Fuck You Till You Love Me: An Anthology of Poems Inspired by Mike Tyson

★ ★ ★

I Was the Most Creative Out of All My Siblings, yet They Are All Doing Better Than Me Financially, Emotionally, Romantically, Etc. Etc.: A Memoir about My Junkyard of Underappreciated Talents

★ ★ ★

Creepily Stalking Your Instagram Stories and Other Stories

★ ★ ★

Even As a Grown-Ass Adult I Nearly Drowned After Walking Drunkenly into a Possibly Alligator-Infested Swamp, and At Any Moment I Feel As Though I Could Definitely Fall into a Gorilla Pit Like That Baby Did, So Who Am I to Judge?: Essays

★ ★ ★

I Have Come Here to Make Insanely Poor Decisions and to Hate Myself... and I Already Hate Myself: Selected Poems

★ ★ ★

I Hold My Head in My Hands and Repeat, "I'm a Human Dumpster Fire...": A Memoir

★ ★ ★

I Think I'd Rather Be Dead: Essays, Interviews, Reviews and Other Mostly Annoying Shit People Have Asked Me to Do

★ ★ ★

Figuring out Life One Totino's® Party Pizza® at a Time: A Foodie's Journey

★ ★ ★

A Portrait of the INFJ as a Young Personality Type and Other Young Personality Types

★ ★ ★

Time Flies When You're Wasting Away on the Internet: Collected URLogies

★ ★ ★

The Amputee's Guide to Sex and the City

★ ★ ★

When Someone Really Likes You but You Can't Totally Like Them Back Because Your Life is a Living Hell Right Now and Inside You are Screaming for Death: Dating Advice for the Recently Soulless

★ ★ ★

Just Give Us Your Money, You Sad Little Bitch: A Poetry Anthology

★ ★ ★

Wake Up Every Morning Feeling Unlucky to Be Alive: An Illustrated History

★ ★ ★

Learn to Be Cool When Things Blow Up in Your Fucking Face: A Self-Help Guide

★ ★ ★

She Loves Weed More Than She Loves Me: A Love Story

* * *

Play It as It Lay's®

* * *

Drunkenly Wandering Through This Dark Year Alone and Into the Next One and Other Stories

* * *

Cryin' While Fuckin': A Sexual Awakening 3

* * *

This is What My Depression Looks Like: Collected Photos of Bathroom/Bedroom Ceilings Taken by People Too Miserable to Get up Off the Floor

* * *

Something Completely Annoying and Wack This Way Comes

* * *

Planning on Dying Broke and Alone? Smash That Like Button: The Unbearable Lightness of Being Online Too Much

* * *

With a Dead Dream in My Heart, Rot in My Soul, and a Can of Pringles® in My Purse: A Traveler's Journey

8. I Love You but I've Chosen Status Update Lit

#TFW you're tempted to ask everyone who's submitted to your journal to re-submit their submissions as MOBI files, just to piss them off.

★ ★ ★

HOT LIT TIP: Never read poems by poets that are about poets/poetry unless the poems are making fun of poets/poetry.

★ ★ ★

Fantasy where you write a Bizarro novella called *Class of Duke Nukem High* and then immediately become king of the Bizarros.

★ ★ ★

Congrats, author, your book is now stocked at a soulless, corporate bookstore chain where you can drink overpriced coffee while pretending to do dumb shit on a laptop/read magazines without having to pay for them.

★ ★ ★

Listening to a dance remix of Willie Nelson's "On the Road Again" > reading Jack Kerouac's *On the Road* again (or ever)

★ ★ ★

♪ For those authors about to open their book with an Ultimate Warrior quote, we salute you. ♪

★ ★ ★

You've probably never felt more alone than in a room full of poets, have you?

★ ★ ★

Author bio: *Seriously, just google me.*

★ ★ ★

Death by guest blogging.

★ ★ ★

"Poets are the absolute worst pieces of trash LOL"

★ ★ ★

★receives Facebook message★

Oh hey, our featured poet got sick. Would be cool if you could read in their place. Let me know!

★deactivates Facebook★

★ ★ ★

A poetry journal that only prints the table of contents page because that's how far most readers get before dying of boredom.

★ ★ ★

Convincing yourself that author Dennis Cooper is really dead and that all the experimental indie writers are just using his name/brand to promote their own books.

★ ★ ★

One thing that's worse than think pieces about the book *Infinite Jest* is the book *Infinite Jest*.

★ ★ ★

Dave & Buster's Realism vs. Family Dollar Realism vs. Cheesecake Factory Realism vs. Bealls Outlet Realism vs. Bed, Bath & Beyond Realism vs. Buffalo Wild Wings Realism

★ ★ ★

notices a sign that says "Meet the Author"

Umm... I'm good.

★ ★ ★

You have an actual office with a chair and a desk!? Several people have written/published books while laying on a mattress covered with old garbage and cat hair, so...

★ ★ ★

Writing prompt:

Pretty sure things went downhill the day Mom threw away my Pog collection...

★ ★ ★

Why not reply to an acceptance from an indie lit journal with: "Cool. Guess this'll do until *The Paris Review* finally recognizes my full potential *sigh*"

★ ★ ★

If anyone in the writing community wonders where you stand on certain topics/politics/controversies, just tell them you exclusively stand by your cats (your actual feline cats, not your hip writer friends), even if that makes you part of the (cat) problem.

★ ★ ★

HOT LIT TIP: Try being the damp dishrag hanging over the edge of the General Fiction section.

★ ★ ★

A Bizarro novella called *Sextraterrestrial*, about someone receiving sexy text messages—but from another planet.

★ ★ ★

HOT LIT TIP: Bring a Sylvia Plath book to the beach with you. Bury your head in the sand. If Cobra Kai show up to fuck with your crush's boom box, don't fight it.

★ ★ ★

How can you be upset that your short stories get rejected when you're constantly rejecting love?

★ ★ ★

You know you hate life when going on an emotionally and financially devastating book tour seems like it'd be a fun/refreshing alternative to whatever rut you're in.

★ ★ ★

You just had lunch at Panera Bread with your agent. JK. You sat in a dark room reviewing your Amazon sales rankings while desperately eating bowls of Fruity Pebbles.

★ ★ ★

"Sorry, what was it you were saying? I was hard at work on 'The Great American Social Media Status.'"

★ ★ ★

A prize presented to you by WWE Superstar Booker T > the Man Booker Prize

★ ★ ★

So you sold your first novel for a used pair of TapouT-brand sneakers, so what?

★ ★ ★

The act of writing described as an "artistic journey" vs. the act of writing described as an "alternative to jumping off of tall structures."

★ ★ ★

Publish first book, your non–lit friends are all: "That's so awesome!" Second book, they're all: "Oh cool." Every book thereafter and it's: "Wait, why are you still doing this to yourself?"

★ ★ ★

Opposite Day Book Reviews: "*War and Peace* is a short, breezy read brimming with funny, relatable characters. Didn't want it to end, honestly!"

★ ★ ★

You may or may not wish to one day write an essay that readers will describe as "gorgeous."

★ ★ ★

"Sorry, your story isn't right for us, so we're going to pass on it. However, we would like to publish your author bio. That shit is funny!"

★ ★ ★

Being a "full-time writer" sounds miserable as fuck.

★ ★ ★

Author bio: *[Insert name] currently survives on Papa John's Pizza and regret.*

★ ★ ★

"You must stay drunk in reality so writing cannot destroy you."—Bae Radbury

★ ★ ★

Dick pics vs. WIP (work-in-progress) pics

★ ★ ★

"If Patty Loveless in her prime isn't pound for pound your all-time favorite poet then see ya later, poser!"

★ ★ ★

Penguin CreateSpace Classics

★ ★ ★

HOT LIT TIP: Never trust anyone who says writing is therapeutic. Never.

★ ★ ★

The Poet Laureate of you're so full of shit.

★ ★ ★

MFA in perpetually forgetting where you left your bicycle locked up while in a drunken stupor.

★ ★ ★

Q: How do you do what you do?

A: Basically I have to search the deepest parts of my being in order to amuse myself while simultaneously seeking validation from strangers because I can't find my place in the world and I constantly want to die. That's how writing works, right?

9. So You Sold Your First Novel For A Previously-Bitten-Into Klondike Bar, So What?

Your Kindle is fucking up, probably because there are too many crappy books on it that you'll never actually read.

★ ★ ★

#TFW you realize how many unsuccessful writers there are who have literary agents, which comes as a shock because you thought all unsuccessful writers were just agent-less pieces of depressed garbage who spent too much time online and didn't get paid good.

★ ★ ★

Emo-revivalist group comprised of twenty-something indie writers called Taking Back Alt-Lit. *fist bump*

★ ★ ★

Free flash fiction writing course: 1.) Start a short story, 2.) quickly get bored with it, and 3) end it as soon as possible.

★ ★ ★

You'll one day get a rejection that begins with "Dear [ ]" and then get a follow-up e-mail from someone apologizing and saying, "I hope this does not arouse any feelings of insignificance," and you will think, *Of course it does, because when I get an automated rejection letter I want someone to take the time to copy and paste my name at the top, goddamn it, just like everyone else's automated rejection letter, even if my name is misspelled, which is common.*

★ ★ ★

Possible sequels to a book titled *King Shit*:

Queen Turd
Prince Crap
Jester Poop

★ ★ ★

Poetry reading where poets read poems in their worst Arnold Schwarzenegger voice.

★ ★ ★

So you sold your first novel for a really bad haircut, so what?

★ ★ ★

You couldn't tell if *Creepshow* was a horror movie or an exposé on the Alt-Lit community's darker elements, could you?

★ ★ ★

Why not publish an oral history about how oral histories suddenly became, like, a thing.

★ ★ ★

Respect if you're currently writing the literary equivalent to an Arby's Beef 'n Cheddar Classic.

★ ★ ★

Maybe she's born with it, maybe her only motivation when having to mail out Advanced Reading Copies of books is that there's an Applebee's Neighborhood Grill & Bar across the street from the post office.

★ ★ ★

Writers' residency where you move back in with your mom after your buddy's horrified reactions to seeing how a writer actually exists in this world took a turn for the worse, and you and your mom argue over what to watch on TV and you don't write anything.

★ ★ ★

Poet-in-Residence @ the job you hate.

★ ★ ★

"Hey normy, stop asking writers about their book sales!"

★ ★ ★

Congratulations! You have a poem in the new issue of not-*The Paris Review*, and a story in the latest not-*The New Yorker*!

★ ★ ★

"What is it about 'people are garbage, my life is decay, fuck this 666' that makes you think I'd actually want to blurb your book?"

★ ★ ★

Q: Where do your story ideas come from?

A: Where do you think they come from? I'm miserable
       and unwell, motherfucker!

★ ★ ★

List of Bands You Didn't Realize Got Their Names from
the Titles of Books Selected for Oprah's Book Club That
They Didn't Bother Reading

★ ★ ★

"You've finally reached the point of gnome return, which
Kafka says is the point that must be reached, so hella
kudos."—Gnome Chomsky

★ ★ ★

Pen name goals: Crocodile Hunter S. Thompson

★ ★ ★

When running your small press that seemingly nobody
but you gives a damn about, it's sometimes easy to forget
that other publishers actually sell books. Like, literally sell
them. Like they print a ton and then sell a ton and then
have to print up another ton to meet some weird, buying-
ass demand. It's so fuckin' wild, man.

★ ★ ★

If you run a journal that doesn't pay writers *and* won't mail
at least one contributor's copy, then you're garbage, which
is fine, garbage rules, just own up to it.

★ ★ ★

There's still time to submit your chapbook!

I mean, kinda... our lives are running out quicker than we think, so...

★ ★ ★

If your submission is accepted but your contact e-mail is BellSouth-affiliated then your bio should automatically be: *[insert author] has a BellSouth e-mail address LOL*

★ ★ ★

Q: How'd the book release party go?

A: Had to leave the house so obviously a complete
        disaster.

★ ★ ★

This Thanksgiving, be thankful to have never been nominated for a Pushcart Prize.

★ ★ ★

Your tax forms are now available for download in your Kindle Direct Publishing account = LOL

★ ★ ★

#TFW you finally find that review of your book on that one blog to use as a blurb but then realize that the review wasn't very good at all.

★ ★ ★

♪ failed at writing and it feels so good ♪ ★in the tune of that "reunited" song★

★ ★ ★

HOT LIT TIP: End every short story with the line: *And that's how I beat Shaq.*

★ ★ ★

Why go on a soul-crushing book tour when you can just head out on a cross-country fast food-tasting excursion?

★ ★ ★

Writing is like sending an SOS out into the world and not quite getting the help you need, if any at all.

★ ★ ★

If being a "literary outsider" means having to write outdoors then sorry, no thanks.

★ ★ ★

The Unbearable Lightness of Being Bogo La Croix

★ ★ ★

Fuck the National Book Award. Fuck the Pulitzer. Why not be the first author to receive a Cheetos endorsement deal?

★ ★ ★

ATTN: Tonight's poetry reading was moved from the main café floor to the employee break room/broom closet. Please clean up after yourself!—MGMT

★ ★ ★

Reminder: Like writers, publishers are comprised of human garbage too.

★ ★ ★

HOT LIT TIP: Never meet your literary heroes, even the ones who already seem like shitty people. It'll only get unimaginably worse. In fact, don't meet anyone ever.

★ ★ ★

#TFW you think about going back to your roots and publishing a zine but then quickly realize all the time you'd have to spend at FedEx and you're like umm no.

★ ★ ★

Sure, go ahead and kill the Classic Novels category on *Jeopardy* while at the bar, like a serious dickhead.

★ ★ ★

ATTN: The reading tonight has been moved to the TGI Fridays down the street. Sorry for the convenience.

10. BRO, DO YOU EVEN READ SUBMISSION GUIDELINES?

Five Rejected Submissions to a 25-Words-Only Short Story Contest

The Face

He made a stupid-ass face.

"Goddamn it, what?" she said. "Am I so heinous you won't snort coke off my titties?"

"I'm hurting," he said.

★ ★ ★

The Joke

If I wrote jokes for comedian Jeff Foxworthy: "If you think broadband is something you tie around your old lady, you might be a redneck."

★ ★ ★

The Decorations

I know she lives in a poor-ass neighborhood, but did they really have to break into Mom's car and steal her Tweety Bird ornaments? Fuck.

★ ★ ★

The Separation

Their stuff is now in two separate piles.
  He wants a kiss.
  "And what," she says, "go and ruin this perfectly good distance we've created?"

★ ★ ★

The Eat-a-Dick

Eventually, the only kinds of women certain men are privy to are those who piss on their floors and tell them to eat a dick.

11. Nu Poetry

People may think pissing your pants at literary readings is "part of the act" when really it's just ill-preparation coupled with not wanting to be there at all.

★ ★ ★

Approaching someone who's just read your book as though you're a waiter politely asking how the meal was.

★ ★ ★

HOT LIT TIP: Immediately tear up any mail you receive that has the word "poetry" written/printed anywhere on the envelope.

★ ★ ★

Title for a novel that starts at a funeral: *It starts at a Funeral.*

★ ★ ★

May is "Short Story Month," meaning it's that time of year when we celebrate all the writers who don't waste everyone's precious time with their shitty poems and/or boring, long-winded novels.

★ ★ ★

If you don't win the contest but the journal wants to publish your story anyway, they *could* just refund you your submission fee, but noooooo...

★ ★ ★

Cause of death: Published via a university press.

★ ★ ★

HOT LIT TIP: Audiences at poetry/literary readings are generally charmed by stuttering, fidgeting, poop talk, apologies, and constant stop-and-starts.

★ ★ ★

So you sold your first novel for a partially scratched CD copy of *Mellon Collie and the Infinite Sadness* that's missing disc 2, so what?

★ ★ ★

Reminder: Self-publish. (Also, self-destruct.)

★ ★ ★

Imagine a revenge horror novel/movie about a writer who stalks then kills a Goodreads troll, called *HemingSLAY: To Kill a Mocking Turd.*

★ ★ ★

HOT LIT TIP: Go ahead and put forehead pentagrams on all your author pictures using Microsoft Paint, even if your mom thinks it's stupid.

★ ★ ★

A List of Books to Read this Month Because if You Read Them Next Month or Even Next Year You Might Not Like Them as Much or Maybe Not At All

★ ★ ★

HOT LIT TIP: Can't land an agent/publicist? Try convincing very drunk people at bars to order your self-published books from their smart phones. Easy.

★ ★ ★

Imagine a movie about a struggling writer who robs a bank and takes Meg Ryan hostage in protest over Tom Hanks getting a lucrative book deal, called *You've Got Mailer*.

★ ★ ★

Jean Genet, immediately after downloading the Pokémon Go app: "To escape the horror, bury yourself in it."

★ ★ ★

Reminder: Pretty much any book that opens with what the weather was like should be thrown in the fucking garbage.

★ ★ ★

Trigger warning: "full-length poetry collection."

★ ★ ★

Using programs like InDesign to layout your book is basic as fuck ★waits for MS Paint to finish loading★

★ ★ ★

Indie publishing is like laughing while throwing money into a dumpster that's been set on fire.

★ ★ ★

What makes for bad writing? Academics who pretentiously write critical, pompous think pieces about "bad writing."

★ ★ ★

Only benefit to "micro-poetry": less poetry.

★ ★ ★

Spitting in your own book before giving it to someone to read as though you're an angry waiter who's been disrespected their entire life.

★ ★ ★

"The Unsung Heroes of the Poetry World" definitely sounds like the tagline to a horror movie.

★ ★ ★

Writer Composed of 50% Water, 30% Self-Delusion and 20% 3 AM Binge Eating/Drinking/Self-Hate/Google Search, Studies Show

★ ★ ★

Reminder: Romanticizing literature is difficult these days, especially when putting together Amazon targeted ad campaigns is pretty much how most writers/publishers suffer for their art.

★ ★ ★

Is Submittable "In Progress" basically like if someone from Domino's takes a really long time to double check for quality but then decides to just throw your pizza in the goddamn trash, or no?

★ ★ ★

You may or may not go on Goodreads often, but when you, do you feel like you're on the deep web and someone is going to show up to your house and kill you?

★ ★ ★

Highly recommend using "poet voice" when ordering Pizza Hut over the phone.

★ ★ ★

Q: Who are your main influences?

A: Oh, you mean like the people responsible for ruining my entire life? Well, let's see...

★ ★ ★

Pick up the nearest book, open it, hawk a loogie into it, slam it shut. This explains nothing 666

★ ★ ★

Randomly getting tagged in someone's Facebook post about their poetry collection may or may not be the worst thing to ever happen to you on the Internet.

* * *

"Sure, newbie writer, I'll help you edit and self-publish your book for free even though I spent 20 years learning how to do it myself without any help…"

* * *

A Goodreads shelf titled "Books I'd Finish Reading if I Wasn't So Whatever about Having to Charge My Kindle."

* * *

Editor: Got a minute to look over these changes we made?

Author: Yeah, yeah, I guess… *pauses random "fails" video on YouTube*

* * *

G.I. Jane Eyre #90sABook

* * *

Intoxicated Writer Sets Literary Agent on Fire While Trying to Light Fart

* * *

#TFW you've almost finished your novel that's pretty much been 10 years in the making and you realize it's not very good but oh wellz LOL

* * *

Poetry reading where you record yourself screaming into a *Home Alone 2* Talkboy then play it back and listen as enchanting poetry fills the room.

★ ★ ★

Have you "made progress" with dissociating from reality on Goodreads?

★ ★ ★

An invisible poem:

★ ★ ★

The Unbearable Lightness of Being a Writer who still Thinks Tumblr is Relevant

★ ★ ★

Dream where you call up Voicemail Poems* and read the lyrics to "Smooth Up In Ya" by BulletBoys**.

★ ★ ★

Poetry reading where you look hip pretending to read your poetry off of a vintage Gameboy that doesn't even work.

*Voicemail Poems is a website where people submit their poems via voicemail.

**BulletBoys is a late '80s hair metal band that nobody remembers.

12. The Art of Storytelling is to Just Lie Your Ass Off

Most writers should just take a break from being writers and develop a debilitating drug habit for a few years, and even then, who the hell knows?

★ ★ ★

Reminder: Every poet is just one chapbook away from ending it all.

★ ★ ★

Depression/anxiety has pretty much ruined everything for you but at least creating all those stories that make very little money is lit af fam LOL

★ ★ ★

Since The Internet Has Now Become an Infinite Black Hole Which Fuels Our Collective Self-Hate, Good Books Are Easier Than Ever To Put Down, Studies Show

★ ★ ★

A Goodreads giveaway where the winners get to choose the exact method in which the author physically destroys copies of his/her own book.

★ ★ ★

Probably the worst aspect of editing an online poetry journal is having to be the person who thought it was a good idea to edit an online poetry journal.

★ ★ ★

HOT LIT TIP: The last sentence of your novel should just be: *Thelma and Louise ending.*

★ ★ ★

Throwing your book in the trash as though you're a waiter who's been confronted by a customer who didn't enjoy their meal and wants a refund.

★ ★ ★

It's highly recommended that writers respond to their rejection letters with: *No, no, better look over it again. I'll wait.*

★ ★ ★

HOT LIT TIP: Instead of writing new books, just keep obsessively revising the old ones until you die.

★ ★ ★

Q: Do you need help building your author platform?

A: Hmm, maybe, but could you get me some good drugs?

★ ★ ★

Your forthcoming nervous breakdown > your forthcoming chapbook

★ ★ ★

Might be cooler if the place in Florida that Kerouac once lived in became a crack house instead of a writers' retreat. Just saying.

★ ★ ★

Authors who say they're all for the First Amendment but then get pissed and start petitioning Amazon to remove negative reviews of their books = LOL

★ ★ ★

If writing every day includes chronicling your various cries for help via Twitter, then congratulations, Hemingway— here's your awesome PEN award!

★ ★ ★

Scribblers & Dribblers > *Poets & Writers*

★ ★ ★

ATTN writers who publish their playlists: Not only does your book put people to sleep but so do those Bon Iver tracks you listened to while writing it.

★ ★ ★

The Da Vinci Code < The cheat code to get to Mike Tyson without having to beat Super Macho Man while playing *Mike Tyson's Punch-Out!!*

* * *

Admit it, if you had to choose between reading something or writing something you'd probably just pick tweeting.

* * *

Oh your word count is pretty solid this evening, writer— now tell us how many of those words will matter once the void swallows you whole?

* * *

Poetry reading where poets read poems like that one kid in class who didn't read well but got asked by the teacher to read aloud anyway.

* * *

Has anyone ever had a pizza delivered to them during a poetry reading, and if not, how come?

* * *

Author picture where the author is photographed while savagely shoving froyo into their face.

* * *

You may or may not have started reading *The Great Gatsby* in high school till the teacher was all fuck it and made everyone just watch the movie and all you remember about it was the scene where Robert Redford gets murdered in a pool.

* * *

Because someone snagged my Cranberries CD from the quad. #WhyIWrite

★ ★ ★

A "Collected Works" comprised of all the old Internet passwords you forgot and had to discard.

★ ★ ★

Need tips on self-publishing your book? Here's a list of shit you can buy from other self-published authors that probably won't help at all!

★ ★ ★

HOT LIT TIP: Planting virtual items throughout your weekly poetry slams to trick unsuspecting Pokémon Go players will increase attendance by maybe 4 or 5 more nerds.

★ ★ ★

Disabling the "Currently Reading" shelf on your Goodreads account but just until your debilitating commitment issues have been resolved.

★ ★ ★

Poetry reading where you read poems collated inside the No Rules! Trapper Keeper you used to carry around in middle school.

★ ★ ★

Poet-in-Residence @ a Checkers drive-thru.

★ ★ ★

Motivating yourself to stuff books into envelopes, address them, and then go to the post office to mail them seems more like a miracle accomplishment than actually writing/ publishing said books.

★ ★ ★

Poetry reading held inside a dumpster.

★ ★ ★

#TFW someone tells you to check out that new movie adaptation of that one book you never read and your eyes glaze over and you want to die but mainly because of other things.

★ ★ ★

The Best of (the movie) The Net

★ ★ ★

Yo, check out this list of tight places to optimistically submit your writing before becoming increasingly miserable when all the rejections roll in!

★ ★ ★

HOT LIT TIP: Image-google "toilets" to help inspire advertising strategies when promoting your book.

★ ★ ★

Hmm, this book looks interesting... ★sees douchey picture of book's author★ ...oh, never mind.

★ ★ ★

Submitted for the approval of the Midnight Society, I call this story: "The Tale of the Notion That Literary Agents May or May Not Be Obsolete"

★ ★ ★

Writers who embrace NaNoWriMo* probably fulfill New Year's resolutions, don't eat garbage and exercise regularly, which is super offensive.

★ ★ ★

Horror story in under 10 words:

The jazz is coming from inside the house!

★ ★ ★

HOT LIT TIP: Pushcart a writer off of a building.

★ ★ ★

Boggles the mind that there aren't any current best-selling literary authors who look and act like Dennis Rodman circa 1997.

★ ★ ★

Your life is in the toilet and you're on an epic drug and alcohol bender so you can definitely do 50,000 words this month. Easy. #NaNoWriMo

★ ★ ★

Indie Lit—because it takes money to make almost no money.

*National Novel Writing Month.

13. PUBLISHING HOUSE NAME GENERATOR

Potential Publishers for Your Shitty Manuscript

Suicidal Cat Pillow Press

★ ★ ★

All My Old Emo Friends Press

★ ★ ★

Reject All Feelings Press

★ ★ ★

My Family Didn't Love Me Enough, So... Press

★ ★ ★

Mom's Been Drinking Again Press

★ ★ ★

You Never Gave Me Back My Smashing Pumpkins Zero T-Shirt Press

★ ★ ★

What Kind of Garbage Are You? Press

★ ★ ★

Depressed Dad Press

★ ★ ★

Kurt Cobain Was a Lil Bitch Press

★ ★ ★

Dude, Where's My Think Piece? Press

★ ★ ★

My Girlfriend Got Pissed and Then Punched Me in the Face on Our Way Home from a Get Up Kids Show Press

★ ★ ★

35 & Still Sleeping on Someone Else's Futon Press

★ ★ ★

It's Just a Phase You're Going Through Press

★ ★ ★

Cloudy with a Slight Chance of God's Dead Press

★ ★ ★

You Call Yourself a Fuckin' Editor? Press

★ ★ ★

Well, *That* Sucked Press

★ ★ ★

I Did My Best and It Just Wasn't Good Enough Press

★ ★ ★

Starving Cat Press

★ ★ ★

If You Don't Get a Severed Ear in the Mail Then It's Just
Not Real Press

★ ★ ★

Maybe Some Blog Will Dig It Press

★ ★ ★

Fuck the World but Wear a Condom Press

★ ★ ★

Amazon Took Most of Our Money LOL Press

★ ★ ★

Contemplating Life One Bag of Chips Ahoy!™ Cookies
at a Time Press

★ ★ ★

Fuck This, I'll Publish It My Damn Self Press

★ ★ ★

New Facebook Mom Press

★ ★ ★

Asking for a... oh wait... Press

★ ★ ★

Damaged People We ❤ Press

★ ★ ★

My Goth Girlfriend's Poster of Tori Amos Breastfeeding a
Pig is Starting to Really Freak Me Out Press

★ ★ ★

Amazin' & Self-Hatin' Press

★ ★ ★

Remember LiveJournal? LOL Press

★ ★ ★

No Hope 4 Humanity Press

★ ★ ★

One Place, One Dream, One Toilet Press

★ ★ ★

Cashing In on Your Nervous Breakdown Press

★ ★ ★

On the Right Path (Towards Oblivion) Press

★ ★ ★

No Gods, No Think Pieces Press

★ ★ ★

Total Dad Move Press

★ ★ ★

Do Emoji Androids Dream of Emoji Sheep? Press

★ ★ ★

Mo Anxiety Mo Self-Loathing Press

★ ★ ★

YESt in Peace Press

★ ★ ★

Fuck You, Paypal Me! Press

★ ★ ★

Trudging Through Life without Anything to Really
Look Forward To Besides Death Press

★ ★ ★

Poetry Sux, Dude! Press

★ ★ ★

Your Mom Likes My LiveJournal Press

★ ★ ★

Halloween Sex Dungeon Press

★ ★ ★

So Many Vanity Projects, So Little Time (and $) Press

★ ★ ★

This is Either Gas or I'm About to Have a Heart Attack
Right Here in the Fucking Public Library Press

★ ★ ★

Documentations of Extreme Psychic Terror Passed Down
Through Generations Press

★ ★ ★

BeDazzled Mustache Press

★ ★ ★

Look, Can't I Just Love You In An Indifferent Way? Press

★ ★ ★

Going Nowhere in Life and It's Hella Chill Press

★ ★ ★

Ugh, Can You Not?? Press

★ ★ ★

These Totino's® Pizza Rolls No Longer Help Press

★ ★ ★

Fuck Books, We Only Care about Death Press

★ ★ ★

Listlessly Stabbing Press

★ ★ ★

The Pain Never Ends but We Keep Trying Press

★ ★ ★

Write Every Day and Still Feel Terrible Press

★ ★ ★

Oh Fuck Oh Damn Please Dear God Fill This Emptiness
Inside Myself Press

★ ★ ★

My Cat Smells Like Pork Lo Mein Press

★ ★ ★

LOL Fuck Everything, Dead Inside Forever 666 Press

14. Good Writing Is the Result of One's Compulsion to Make Bad Decisions, or Something

It's easy to tell which writers bought their 10K+ Twitter followers, especially if they're poets 'cause nobody seriously cares that much about poetry.

★ ★ ★

Dear Editor,

Was initially happy about the acceptance but then I saw your journal only has 97 Facebook likes and 61 Twitter followers, so...

★ ★ ★

A fun thing to do: crash a poetry reading naked, smear shit everywhere, punch someone in the face, shout, "I'm GG Allen Ginsberg, motherfucker!" and then leave.

★ ★ ★

Pretty sure that poets and people who are really into porn are the only ones still using Tumblr.

★ ★ ★

Jean Genet, immediately after posting about the *Ghostbusters* reboot on a message board: "To escape the horror, bury yourself in it."

★ ★ ★

Sorry, but the fact that you're asking people to pay money to submit to your bullshit chapbook contest is not "exciting news."

★ ★ ★

♪ Novel of mine, tell me where have you been ♪ ★in the tune of that Everclear song about the shitty dad★

★ ★ ★

Happy birthday [insert literary journal/press], I'm surprised you haven't already folded under the weight of indifference.

★ ★ ★

Don't worry, the folks who reject your work are probably just a bunch of pretentious a-holes sitting around reading Eudora Welty or some shit.

★ ★ ★

Writing a novel then finding an agent to sell your novel is the new "Well, all my friends are settling down and getting married and having kids, so..."

★ ★ ★

Authors/Publishers, why not subtitle your books using the word "dank"? Like, "A Dank Novel," "A Dank Memoir," "Dank Poems," etc. etc. Dank as fuck.

★ ★ ★

Reminder: If a poem doesn't replicate the urgency of a crazy person angrily shouting their order at a Burger King drive-thru then ultimately it fails.

★ ★ ★

[Insert pretentious word that nobody can pronounce/doesn't really exist]: A Journal of Asshole Poets

★ ★ ★

Those Who Read Books Live Longer Than Those Who Don't Yet Those Who Write/Publish Books Will Probably Die Bitter, Broke and Alone, Studies Show

★ ★ ★

Unsolicited writing critiques vs. unsolicited dick pics vs. get u an editor who does both?

★ ★ ★

Dialogue from a draft to a screenplay called *Best Buy Parking Lot*, which was started while purchasing a new computer and dying a little in the process:

All those new, fancy-ass origami-like touch-screen computers suck shit! They don't belong in this world—they belong on fuckin' Mars, man! They can all go to hell, as far as I'm concerned...

★ ★ ★

♪ Hello unsolicited poetry manuscript my old friend ♪

★ ★ ★

It's almost impossible for an author to take an author photo that doesn't make them look like a terribly sad and desperate person.

★ ★ ★

♪ Proof your book, I just can't proof your book ♪ *to the tune of Debbie Gibson's "Shake Your Love"*

★ ★ ★

With slim poetry collections being as expensive as they are, the handful of people who actually read poetry must *really* fucking like it.

★ ★ ★

Hobbies include: browsing all the writers you follow on social media like it's some super sad baseball card collection scattered across a carpeted floor.

★ ★ ★

Most literary podcasts should just be called *Listen as Two Writers Try Boring the Fuck out of Each Other.*

★ ★ ★

HOT LIT TIP: Don't do interviews to promote your writing; do them to promote the fact that you are an emotionally wounded person in need of a temporary friend.

★ ★ ★

Opening to dream blurb: *Not since Springsteen...*

* * *

The term "Publishing House" might be too grand, so how about: "Apartment Overrun By Cat Puke-Covered Boxes of Books I'm Trying to Get a Mostly Illiterate/Indifferent Public to Buy"?

* * *

Might be cool if Twitter started nominating for the Pushcart Prize.

* * *

#TFW it's time to mail books out to those ungrateful piece-of-shit Goodreads contest winners. *sigh*

* * *

Books about professional wrestlers > generally any book not about professional wrestlers

* * *

Time to work on a new manuscript! *rummages through trash can*

* * *

Invaluable dialogue prompt for your story/novel:

She said, "Pretty sad knowing the only reason I ever feel like getting up off the couch is to pee."

"Whatever," he said. "Just piss the couch. It'll be fine."

"If I ever get to that point then I just shouldn't be alive," she said. *"You'd have to kill me."*

"Great," he said. *"I'm already at that point, and you obviously know what to do, so your move."*

★ ★ ★

When another author asks you to trade/review/blurb one of his/her books, it feels like you've been subjected to a Smirnoff Icing challenge.

★ ★ ★

Look, it's okay to feel bad for the co-worker at the Christmas party who received a copy of *Infinite Jest* as their Secret Santa gift.

★ ★ ★

Poetry reading where it's mandatory you tape your fists then place them in a bowl of broken glass before going up to read à la Van Damme movies.

★ ★ ★

HOT LIT TIP: Roll up to your reading with a boom box. Right before you read, ask the audience, "Ya'll ready for this?" Then press Play on the boom box, and stand there expressionless as the first 20 seconds of "Ya'll Ready for This (*Space Jam* Theme)" plays. After that first 20 seconds, "accidentally" drop your boom box, which will hopefully break for effect, and mutter, "Shit," while kicking the broken boom box pieces under someone in the front row's seat. That's your opener. Now start reading.

★ ★ ★

The book *The Perks of Being a Wallflower* should just be called *The Sad Kid with The Dead Aunt Wishes He Had a Friend.*

★ ★ ★

As important in literature as it is in life: Only associate with the best weirdos and losers.

★ ★ ★

Because I'm a narcissistic misanthrope in desperate need of misguided validation while simultaneously drowning in the muck of reality. #WhyIWrite

★ ★ ★

Consider ~~the Lobster~~ Red Lobster

★ ★ ★

Ah, it's time to construct another elaborate e-mail to someone very nice, explaining to them why you're pretty much a complicated piece of garbage who can only fully commit to unreasonable situations that are emotionally damaging to yourself and others. #amwriting

★ ★ ★

Reminder: Literature needs to constantly be destroyed then jerry-rigged back together using gum/glue/safety pins/etc. etc. by someone with their ass crack showing.

15. Pop-Tart Prize > Pushcart Prize

Poetry reading where you refuse to use the house mic and bust out a Toys 'R Us I Am T-Pain Auto Tune Mic, instead.

★ ★ ★

Tagline for a revenge horror novel/movie called *HemingSLAY: To Kill a Mocking Turd*: "A Defamation of SCARE-actor!"

★ ★ ★

Poet-in-Residence @ the part in the movie *Heathers* where the big girl in the "Big Fun" t-shirt purposefully walks into oncoming traffic.

★ ★ ★

So you sold your first novel for an empty Ellio's Pizza box with a cut-out *Teenage Mutant Ninja Turtles* mask on the back, so what?

★ ★ ★

Congratulations to *Ghostbusters* (2016) for receiving the Nobel Prize in Literature! Well deserved.

★ ★ ★

MFA in Fruity Pebbles consumption.

★ ★ ★

Amazon Echo: When you check your Amazon sales and you're all, "Any money in there?" and you just hear your voice reverberate 'cause shit's empty.

★ ★ ★

#TFW you're reading a book where, judging from the glossary, the pages about Waylon Jennings doing cocaine far outnumber the pages about cocaine itself, which means the importance of cocaine is measured by whether or not Waylon Jennings is using it.

★ ★ ★

Would David Foster Wallace embrace the man bun if he were alive today—infinite yes or infinite maybe?

★ ★ ★

Should you call your new fantasy/adventure novel *Dragons and Shit*? Or how about *Baewulf*? Or do you have no legit interest in fantasy, adventure, or novels?

★ ★ ★

Ending to a short story about a guy who goes to a CVS to buy a belated Mother's Day card and is thrown shade by the cashier for being a shitty son causing said shitty son to lose his shit thus ensuing an embarrassing yet heart-breaking scene of love and redemption:

And it wasn't until he was at home and on the toilet readying to wipe his ass that he realized he'd left his mother's card on the CVS counter.

★ ★ ★

Book blurbs are like favors. Like giving someone a lift somewhere, or feeding their pets when they're away. Like saying, "I love you," when really you're all, "Eh."

★ ★ ★

Nietzsche the German philosopher vs. Nietzsche the EDM DJ

★ ★ ★

The fact that Kerouac was a fall-down drunk almost makes him likeable. Almost.

★ ★ ★

Reminder: "What's everyone reading right now?" is a regrettable question.

★ ★ ★

Poetry reading held inside one of the shittier $5 DVD bins at Walmart.

★ ★ ★

Book launch party where you just read the book blurbs your "friends" wrote for you as a solid.

★ ★ ★

Writers' retreat where you're the one who's been drunkenly smearing feces all over the stucco walls/ceiling.

★ ★ ★

Hobbies include: Going to a library/book store and reading the first paragraph of a popular novel, saying "Oh fuck you" to it, then putting it back on the shelf.

★ ★ ★

Book club where we discuss Kurt Cobain-related conspiracy theories while wearing Kurt Cobain-related sweaters and drinking Courtney Love-related hunch punch.

★ ★ ★

MFA in creative hiding.

★ ★ ★

You probably don't have a literary agent, but maybe what you *do* have is a personality that tells all your other, more destructive personalities to just chill the fuck out.

★ ★ ★

Okay, but who won the Nobel Prize in Twitterature?

★ ★ ★

Hobbies include: Applying for grants to fund Patrick Swayze-inspired fan fiction journal called *Roadhouse Review*.

★ ★ ★

We read books for fun, sure, but to also give the voices inside our heads something else to talk about besides random episodes of *Full House*.

★ ★ ★

Writers shouldn't waste time developing their characters because people are garbage pretty much always/forever.

★ ★ ★

Roll up to a literary workshop retreat all: "I thought this was supposed to be like *Rock of Love with Bret Michaels,* what the shit??"

★ ★ ★

MFA in kind of knowing how to play the Stone Temple Pilots song "Plush" on an acoustic guitar that's missing a bottom E string.

★ ★ ★

When doing sit-ups you should really strive for that Hemingway tightness… but in regards to abs, not prose.

★ ★ ★

Poetry reading held inside a locked car with the windows rolled up in July.

★ ★ ★

Writers' retreat where you try beating really hard NES games like *Super Contra* and *Kid Icarus* and you don't think about writing at all.

★ ★ ★

The audio version of your book can just be the sound of heavy breathing followed by the sound of muffled sobbing followed by a muzak version of that one Adele song then repeated to fill up several cassette tapes 'cause you're old school like that.

★ ★ ★

Q: Two nuns and a penguin approach you at a bar, and you tell them you're a writer. When they ask you what you write about, how do you answer?

A: I'd be scared if that happened and I'd probably just shriek, "But I'm a writer!" while gradually creeping towards the exit. If they managed to ask what I write about before I made it out alive I would probably shout, "Escaping!" which is generally the most honest answer I could come up with even under regular circumstances.

★ ★ ★

You think it would've been easier for Luke Skywalker to become a certified Jedi if he had first gotten an MFA degree?

★ ★ ★

Admit it, you're kind of an asshole if you celebrate your book's "birthday."

★ ★ ★

A lot of writers find Bob Dylan undeserving of a Nobel Prize for Literature because they feel he isn't one of them, which is true because Dylan doesn't have a blog or a Submittable account or a weekly poetry slam.

★ ★ ★

Every writer's goal should be to one day write a *New York Times* Best Seller entitled *Oh Fuck You.*

★ ★ ★

Sounds crazy, but retreats *from* writers' retreats, you know, just screams "Better deal!"

★ ★ ★

Opening line to your future memoir:

My life fell apart so I moved into subsidized housing with my mom.

★ ★ ★

♪ Anna Karenina, are you okay? Are you okay? Are you okay, Anna?♪ ★in the tune of Alien Ant Farm's cover of Michael Jackson's "Smooth Criminal"★

★ ★ ★

This Father's Day, treat Dad to a copy of one of your books so he can face those abandonment issues he's instilled in you over the years head-on.

★ ★ ★

Writing—or any kind of art, really—is basically just someone being empowered by their own bullshit.

16. AWP IS FUCKING DOG SHIT

A Guide to the Association of Writers and Writing Programs Conference

A shocking number of carnies at the AWP book fair have MFA degrees.

★ ★ ★

Kickstarter to fund an AWP book fair dunk tank.

★ ★ ★

A fun thing to do at AWP: Approach writers you've known for years online but have not met IRL and horribly mispronounce their names.

★ ★ ★

Show you mean business at AWP by randomly approaching someone and very menacingly saying, "We can do this the easy way, or we can do this the Hemingway."

★ ★ ★

An AWP panel titled "Short Stories Mansplained."

★ ★ ★

At AWP, drunk writers have been known to throw entire Twitter posts out of hotel room windows.

★ ★ ★

AWP is where writers spend several days pretending to admire each other's work while drunk as shit.

★ ★ ★

When at AWP, a productive thing to do is to frantically ask random people if they know what time Smash Mouth goes on.

★ ★ ★

A lot of people wear lanyards at AWP, which begs the question: How has nobody at AWP been strangled to death?

★ ★ ★

Mom says I can only swim in the shallow end, so AWP here I come!

★ ★ ★

Look, they were already dead when I got there. #AWP

★ ★ ★

Self-publishing is cool because instead of going to AWP to promote your books, you can just stay home and stream all five Leprechaun sequels on Netflix, your reason being: "Well, I'm just waiting until AWP is in either 'the Hood' or in 'Space.'"

★ ★ ★

An AWP panel titled "How to Remind People That You're an Actual Author and Not Just Some Crazy Depressed Person Who Spends Too Much Time Online."

★ ★ ★

Roll up into AWP ready to pick up some "strange" using literary-themed negs, like "I'd like to stick my head in *your* oven," or "How about a Moby Dick pic?"

★ ★ ★

The best AWP offsite event is where you lay on your shitty mattress staring into nothing while thousands of miles away from any writer.

★ ★ ★

Best thing to pack for AWP? Tissues—to plug into your ears when all those writers try telling you about their "work in progress."

★ ★ ★

Come see us sitting here picking our noses while silently screaming at table 666 #AWP

★ ★ ★

You should oppose AWP because why support organizations which benefit from the sad delusions of lonely, broken people AKA authors/publishers?

★ ★ ★

Most overheard conversation while at AWP:

Person 1:   Wait, who are you?

Person 2:   *says name*

Person 1:   Hmm... *awkward silence*

Person 2:   I've been published in your journal.

Person 1:   Oh. Sorry, I don't remember.

★ ★ ★

Did you know that wearing an AWP badge will automatically get you backstage at a Decemberists show?

★ ★ ★

So is AWP just like a big photo hunt for really boring-ass looking people, or what?

★ ★ ★

AWP panel that's just you sitting in a corner, softly humming/singing the *Degrassi: The Next Generation* theme song while rocking back and forth.

★ ★ ★

A cool thing to do while browsing a table of books at AWP is to just stand there checking Amazon on your phone for better deals.

★ ★ ★

If you actually attend AWP, your main concern should not be to mingle with bullshit writers/publishers/agents but to find the person with the best drugs.

★ ★ ★

At AWP, start a scandalous rumor that your favorite writer was born during a stop on the 1998 KoRn Family Values Tour.

★ ★ ★

AWP Fatal Four Way Buried Alive match in which the loser is smothered under crushed dreams, bumper stickers that say "#amwriting," and Advance Reading Copies of shitty books.

★ ★ ★

Next time you're at AWP, make sure you go up to the Two Dollar Radio booth and politely ask them to turn down the volume on their books.*

★ ★ ★

Reminder: Following AWP you will never want to hear the words "program," "panel," and "mentor" spoken ever again.

★ ★ ★

Skip the AWP conference altogether so you can stay at home tweaking the script for the movie you've titled AWP (*Alien Watches Predator*), which is just the alien from Alien sitting on a couch eating pizza and talking mad shit about Arnold Schwarzenegger's man-growls.**

---

*Two Dollar Radio is a small press which boasts that their books are "too loud to Ignore."

**You play the alien.

17. Listlessly Judge Random Author Bios and Chill?

Indie Lit: "Books" you see people posting about on the Internet that you only assume are real because you never see people reading them IRL.

★ ★ ★

Reminder: It's all fun and games until some asshole writer has to shamelessly promote their new book.

★ ★ ★

Game show where contestants have to determine if a random meta term is the title to a poetry chapbook or the name of some indie band/album.

★ ★ ★

Litcoin: When you let journals publish your writing for free in hopes the "exposure" will lead to bigger and better things that don't really exist.

★ ★ ★

Is getting *Small Press as Fuck* tattooed in Papyrus lettering on your chest a good idea, or no?

★ ★ ★

A "Collected Works" comprised of just the massive debt you've accrued while trying to earn your MFA.

★ ★ ★

Poet: Okay, now I'm going to read you something dark and angst-filled off of my smart phone which my parents pay a lot of money for.

★ ★ ★

Just assume literary journals that only accept postal submissions this day and age are run by people who self-identify as "steampunk."

★ ★ ★

Finishing wrestling move where you devastate your opponent by Facebook-inviting them to your poetry reading.

★ ★ ★

Jean Genet, immediately after sharing the Chewbacca Mom video: "To escape the horror, bury yourself in it."

★ ★ ★

Dream where you get a rejection letter that thanks you for submitting your manuscript and then tells you to burn in hell.

★ ★ ★

The "old man" in Ernest Hemingway's *The Old Man and The Sea* is actually Doc Brown, and the boat is actually a DeLorean, and the sea is time, and Moby Dick is really the sports almanac Biff stole from the future.

★ ★ ★

J.D. Salinger is the literary equivalent of Michael Jackson—if you replace Macaulay Culkin with Joyce Maynard, and the Jackson family with World War II.

★ ★ ★

Poetry reading that is actually called a "floatetry" reading, because someone read their poems from inside an inner tube while at a water park.

★ ★ ★

"While My ~~Guitar~~ Amazon Sales Ranking Gently Weeps"

★ ★ ★

Good news: Your book just went into its third printing—meaning the book is print-on-demand and only three people have purchased it.

★ ★ ★

"Sorry, but you lost me with your Kerouac fascination."

★ ★ ★

Status: Currently revising your latest ~~bad relationship~~ novel.

★ ★ ★

To be a writer you'll need two of the following forms of ID: MFA; substance abuse problem; eating disorder; weird upbringing; inherent dislike towards people coupled with a somewhat disturbing reverence for your pet(s); twitter account.

★ ★ ★

Writers are generally so desperate that you'll often wonder how many of them, if guaranteed an agent/lucrative book deal, would join ISIS.

★ ★ ★

Choose Your Own Literary Reading Adventure: A. Arrive late. B. Don't show. C. Be the one to ask, "Can you read first? My friends aren't here yet."

★ ★ ★

Oh, weird, another indie publishing press did something stupid that pissed some people off, as if publishing books that don't make any money isn't stupid enough.

★ ★ ★

Yeah, but when is Self-Published Books Nobody Wants Week?

★ ★ ★

When u a rich white writer and u run out of ideas and consider writing about murdering your rich white writer friends but think lol nah.

★ ★ ★

Books for [insert season] that You Can Maybe Shelve on Goodreads but Probably Won't Bother to Actually Buy/Read

★ ★ ★

You might be a white male writer if... you have an MFA; wear only earth tones; host a podcast; keep a well-groomed beard; should maybe stop writing.

★ ★ ★

Would The Plot Hole be a good name for a literary-themed strip club, or no?

★ ★ ★

Did you know you were allowed to karate chop writers who distribute business cards advertising the fact that they are writers?

★ ★ ★

The 10 Best Books Shorter Than 150 Pages but Longer Than 112 Pages

★ ★ ★

Penn & Teller > PEN/Faulkner

★ ★ ★

HOT LIT TIP: If a publishing house is willing to print your books out on rolls of toilet paper, sign with them immediately.

★ ★ ★

Forever searching for the literary equivalent to the movie
Snow Day.

★ ★ ★

When you've just started getting published and are revising
an author biography, resist the urge of sarcastically listing
journals that have rejected your work, even if those credits
far outnumber the places which *have* accepted it. This ratio
will never change. Ever. No matter how many acceptances
you receive. No matter how many prizes you win. So just
stop. Just fucking stop.

★ ★ ★

When you have anxiety about going to a poetry/literary
reading and you're not even the one reading.

★ ★ ★

Dream where you're a Fantasy writer who is dressed like a
knight in an author photo.

★ ★ ★

ATTN: Depressed of the Net nominations are now open.

★ ★ ★

#TFW you suddenly feel that not using the pen name
"Karl Withers" was a big missed opportunity.

★ ★ ★

It takes, like, two minutes to submit writing to a literary journal... and a lifetime to get over the rejection.

★ ★ ★

Writer quip: *Look, I didn't open a Submittable account yesterday, buddy...*

★ ★ ★

Pulitzer Prize in getting dumped via text.

★ ★ ★

ATTN: Please donate to our dumb-ass literary journal you don't really care about that'll eventually fold regardless of whether you donate or not.

★ ★ ★

MTV True Life: My Crazy-Ass Cousin Wants Me to Co-Write His Memoir

★ ★ ★

The thing about poetry is that writing a poem only seems like a good idea at the time but then oh boy.

★ ★ ★

Writers are like the vegans of art, in the sense that they need to brag about it to people who don't really care at all.

★ ★ ★

Hell is other people's use of famous author quotes.

★ ★ ★

As an act of solidarity, writers should all quit and get, like, seriously addicted to online poker, or maybe bingo.

★ ★ ★

RIP status update lit.

18. It's Crazy, Sure, but Form Rejections Should Feel like Home

Think of writing/publishing as just your little hobby until you eventually die broke and alone.

★ ★ ★

Who are your favorite writers that ~~haven't gone to college or have an MFA~~ didn't go see the first *Teenage Mutant Ninja Turtles* film opening weekend?

★ ★ ★

Writing prompt:

"That's the last time you ever embarrass me at a Zaxby's," she cried...

★ ★ ★

HOT LIT TIP: When stumbling upon a "What's everyone reading?" message board thread, use one finger to scroll through it as quickly as possible while using another finger to pick your nose.

★ ★ ★

Composing yet another elaborate e-mail that's again basically an apology to someone for you being a shitty dumpster fire of a human being. #amwriting

★ ★ ★

When you find someone's recent bank receipt in a book you've checked out from the library, consider lightly stalking them online because the book might be really good and of course you'd love to get their opinion on it.

★ ★ ★

"Owner at Self-Employed" is person who randomly follows you on social media's main bitch; "Works at Author" is person who randomly follows you on social media's side bitch.

★ ★ ★

The hope that writers/publishers have finally come to realize that Goodreads book giveaways are strictly for amateurs and masochists.

★ ★ ★

Keep writing so as to live your shitty dream that one day your art will be misunderstood by lots and lots of people, not just a few.

★ ★ ★

Author pen name/rap name: Submittable Killah

★ ★ ★

Trigger warning: "National Poetry Month"

★ ★ ★

When is National Status Update Lit Month?

★ ★ ★

Writing prompt:

One time we were going through a McDonald's drive-thru and...

★ ★ ★

RIP the writers you thought you knew who all stopped creating and just started posting political rants on social media every day.

★ ★ ★

Does "...a major voice in southern literature" just mean "...this person writes real good about poor white trash," or no?

★ ★ ★

Are your books print-on-demand? If so, then understand that the spine will be completely fucked up on almost every other book ordered.

★ ★ ★

HOT LIT TIP: Design your books using a free trial of Microsoft Word, setting the text in whichever fonts are offered besides Comic Sans or Wingdings.

★ ★ ★

If you don't consider yourself the "Poet Laureate of garbage set on fire" then see ya later!

★ ★ ★

Author's co-worker: You excited about your novel coming out?

Author: *shrugs* Eh, not really.

Author's co-worke: Oh.

★ ★ ★

Master at writing phat lines < master at snorting fat lines

★ ★ ★

Fantasy about one day becoming a famous writer < Fantasy about one day becoming a bed-ridden invalid who gets hand jobs via a fat nurse

★ ★ ★

Reminder: Writing is a horror show and the bone-chilling disaster that is your unfinished novel is coming from inside the house...

★ ★ ★

Facebook User who "Works at Writer" Wonders Why W-2 Has Yet to Arrive

★ ★ ★

HOT LIT TIP: Dedicate your next book to Camel Crush.

★ ★ ★

HOT LIT TIP: Get so drunk at your next reading that someone has to put your ass in an Uber that miraculously drops you off at Waffle House.

★ ★ ★

Author's fantasy about one day being interviewed by Charlie Rose < Author's fantasy about one day being interviewed by a crazy person who wears a paper bag on their head

★ ★ ★

If updating your author CV doesn't entail scribbling furiously on a Taco Bell napkin then see ya later!

★ ★ ★

HOT LIT TIP: Remind editors to nominate your unwavering paranoia for a Pushcart this year.

★ ★ ★

Pen name goals: Prosey O'Donnell

★ ★ ★

Coming to Facebook soon on Further Weirding out My Family and Friends Press!

★ ★ ★

♪ Is it worth it? Let me workshop it / I put my MFA down, flip it and reverse it ♪

★ ★ ★

Being in a happy relationship is just part of the work you put into your writing craft before things eventually fall apart and you can finally write about how miserable the relationship actually was.

★ ★ ★

"I don't like showering, but I like having showered."— Dorothy Parker

★ ★ ★

Write how you want, edit how you want, just please stop quoting Hemingway.

★ ★ ★

HOT LIT TIP: Tell people that interviewing you for their literary blog will mean increased web traffic, more ad revenue, street cred, and maybe even the probable birth of a real gnarly looking Pug.

★ ★ ★

Author: Bad dog! ★swats self with rolled up copy of *The New Yorker*★

★ ★ ★

Where the Wild Things Are < "Where the down boys go"— Warrant, "Down Boys"

★ ★ ★

Post on social media about a short story you had published = *cricket sounds* vs. Post on social media about having to clean up vomit at work = *like button gets smashed*

★ ★ ★

"Glowing" book reviews are kind of annoying.

★ ★ ★

Instead of "Break a leg!" wish a writer luck by saying to them, "Pull the trigger, Hemingway!" or "Stick your head in the oven, Sylvia!" or "Drop dead on a boat with a drink in your hand, McCullers!"

★ ★ ★

You may or may not regret admitting on a literary podcast that you generally prefer hand jobs while getting your butthole fingered over having regular sex.

★ ★ ★

Dedicating your book to an actual person instead of, say, Great Value Mac & Cheese, or the Ghostface mask from the 1996 film *Scream*, or a dead professional wrestler, or even a crumpled paper bag tucked into the corner of a dusty room, was a huge mistake, but we're only human, so what do you say we all take a moment to forgive ourselves, huh?

★ ★ ★

Reminder: being interviewed on a podcast by a woman wearing a hand puppet clearly means your literary career has taken a turn for the best.

★ ★ ★

Look, you haven't *really* found your literary voice until it sounds like the muffled screams of someone smashing a pillow into their face.

★ ★ ★

If your author CV isn't just a sopping wet piece of paper that's been carefully unfolded then see ya later!

★ ★ ★

Reminder: Whenever editors revising your story ask you "But what did it smell like?" the answer is always "Garbage. Everything in this world reeks of rotting garbage."

★ ★ ★

Editor: Receiving submissions is fine. I mean, it's always nice as a writer to see what other people are doing... like, besides slowly dying. Those little postcards from hell are really something, you know?

★ ★ ★

Your "writer's journey" may or may not have begun, coincidentally, at the Journeys in the mall where you bought some sick Sketchers that one time.

★ ★ ★

Listening to most literary podcasts is like spending an hour eavesdropping on two boring people having a conversation at Starbucks.

★ ★ ★

HOT LIT TIP: Pull an Andy Kaufman and bring the four or five folks who bother showing up to your reading to IHOP for "free" pancakes and then just ghost them on the bill.

★ ★ ★

Who are your favorite writers that ~~haven't gone to college or have an MFA~~ didn't cry when Ultimate Warrior defeated Hulk Hogan for the WWF title at Wrestlemania VI?

★ ★ ★

Did you even read "Cat Person," bro?

★ ★ ★

Reminder: All your favorite male authors were mama's boys.

★ ★ ★

Some days you're just tempted to throw the Poetry A-K section out into the middle of the street and go work for a Barnes & Noble.

★ ★ ★

Reminder: Books are like people—there are too many and most are garbage but we keep producing them because maybe a really amazing one will turn up though it's doubtful as fuck.

"There are many more writing hints I could share with you, but suddenly I am run over by a truck."

– Michael O'Donoghue

BRIAN ALAN ELLIS runs House of Vlad Productions, and is the author of three novellas, three short-story collections, a previous book of humorous non-fiction, and *Something to Do with Self-Hate*, a novel. His writing has appeared at *Juked, Hobart, Monkeybicycle, Electric Literature, Vol. 1 Brooklyn, Funhouse, Talking Book,* and *Queen Mob's Tea House*, among other places. He lives in Florida, and tweets sad and clever things at both @brianalanellis and @HouseofVlad.

OFFICIAL

CCM ◖

GET OUT OF JAIL
✳ VOUCHER ✳

- -

Tear this out.
Skip that social event.
It's okay.
You don't have to go if you don't want to. Pick up
the book you just bought. Open to the first page.
You'll thank us by the third paragraph.

If friends ask why you were a no-show, show them
this voucher.
You'll be fine.

- -

We're coping.

CPSIA information can be obtained
at www.ICGtesting.com
Printed in the USA
FSHW012142021218
54197FS